Once Upon a Time in Cyberspace

by Sonia Evans
illustrated by Heather Holbrook

Harcourt
SCHOOL PUBLISHERS

Printed in China

ISBN 10: 0-15-350785-3
ISBN 13: 978-0-15-350785-4

Ordering Options
ISBN 10: 0-15-350601-6 (Grade 4 On-Level Collection)
ISBN 13: 978-0-15-350601-7 (Grade 4 On-Level Collection)
ISBN 10: 0-15-357922-6 (package of 5)
ISBN 13: 978-0-15-357922-6 (package of 5)

4 5 6 7 8 9 10 0940 12 11 10 09

Characters

DAN

ELLEN

SPOTTY THE HORSE

PENNY, *Dan and Ellen's 8-year-old daughter*

ZEKE, *a neighbor*

UNCLE RICHARD

AUNT MARTHA

SETTING: A barn

DAN:

Ellen, I thought this horseshoe would help.

Instead it made our horse cry and yelp.

ELLEN:

What's wrong? It doesn't fit quite right?

Go check the size on their Web site.

DAN:

The Internet? As you well know,

that's not a place where I will go!

ELLEN:

Why not? It's full of information.

It can help you in this situation.

DAN:

You know I do things with my hands.

Computers will not plow my lands.

ELLEN:

Just this once can't you give it a try?

You might find some new horseshoes to buy!

DAN:

Maybe for a minute, that is all.

Then I have to clean the stall.

ELLEN:

There you go. Now click that link.

(DAN *clicks the mouse, then smiles.*)

DAN (*Happily*)**:**

This is not so bad, I think!

ELLEN:

Now there's the page that you should read.

It tells all about horseshoes and feed.

DAN:

Why that's the knowledge that I need!

(*Suddenly there is a loud noise and puff of smoke where* DAN *was sitting. When the smoke clears,* DAN *is missing.* ELLEN *searches the room.*)

ELLEN:

Dan? Dan? You're gone, I fear.

A moment ago you were right here.

(PENNY *runs into the room.*)

ELLEN (*Sadly*):

Daddy's gone without a trace!

I think he's gone to cyberspace.

(PENNY *looks at the computer and nods her head.* ZEKE *rushes into the room.*)

ZEKE:

What's going on? I heard a blast.

I rode my horse here really fast.

PENNY (*Pointing to computer*):

My dad has gone inside of this.

It's as if he ceases to exist.

ZEKE (*Examining the computer*):
Now, Penny, dear, you must not pout.
We'll open this and get him out.
ELLEN:
Zeke, you know he's not in there.
He's in the Internet somewhere.
ZEKE (*Confused*):
You say he's caught inside a net?
Some fisher has him, I just bet!
ELLEN:
Your silly ways have helped me see.
I think I know where Dan might be.
If he's stuck out in cyberspace.
He'll go to some familiar place.

ELLEN:

Let's think of things Dan likes to do.

Then we'll search a site or two.

ZEKE:

Dan and I, we love to fish.

To catch the big one, that's our wish!

(ELLEN *types on the keyboard and clicks the mouse.*)

ELLEN:

This Web site sells good hooks and poles.

ZEKE:

I don't see any fishing holes.

ELLEN:

OK, then let us search some more.

Perhaps he isn't in a store.

(ELLEN *types and clicks some more.*)

ELLEN:

Here: A Web site of a lake.

ZEKE (*Yelling fiercely*)**:**

Dan, come out for goodness sake!

(AUNT MARTHA *and* UNCLE RICHARD *enter the room.*)

ELLEN (*To* AUNT MARTHA):

Your darling nephew, Dan, is lost!

AUNT MARTHA:

We must find him at any cost!

ELLEN:

He's on the Web. That much we know.

Where do you think that he might go?

AUNT MARTHA (*Holding up a coffee cup*):

I know he likes his coffee.

He drinks it from this cup.

Perhaps he's on some Web site

where they're brewing coffee up.

ELLEN:

I'm impressed! Your brain is on!

Let's go to coffeecups.rom.

(ELLEN *clicks and types as the others stare at the screen.*)

ZEKE:

You say that Dan is in a coffee cup?

He must have had to fold his long legs up!

UNCLE RICHARD:

He's not there. He got a cup to go.

Dan doesn't waste much time, you know.

ELLEN:

You're his uncle. You know what he's like.

Where on the Web do you think Dan might hike?

UNCLE RICHARD:

He likes to read about times of the past.

In an encyclopedia, he'd have a real blast.

He could read about ancient history and such.

For him, no amount of information is too much.

PENNY:

Mom, just do a search. It beats looking around.

ELLEN:

I typed in his name. It said, "No entries found."

ZEKE:

Who is "entries"? We're looking for Dan.

UNCLE RICHARD:

Please leave now, Zeke, my good man.

(ZEKE *leaves.*)

(ZEKE *is walking past DAN's barn on his way home. The barn door is open.*)

SPOTTY THE HORSE (*From inside the barn*)**:**

Hey, Zeke!

(ZEKE *looks toward the barn, sees no one, and keeps walking.*)

SPOTTY THE HORSE (*Sticking his head out of the barn door*)**:**

Zeke, come this way as you walk,

and you shall meet a horse that can talk.

ZEKE:

Spotty? You speak? I never knew!

SPOTTY THE HORSE:

Well, I never felt like talking to you.

10

SPOTTY THE HORSE:

Tonight there's something that I must say.

Where do people go at the end of the day?

Where do folks go when they need to rest?

The answer is easy: They go back to their nest.

(ZEKE *just stares at* SPOTTY THE HORSE, *totally confused.*)

SPOTTY THE HORSE:

Don't you get it, Zeke? I'm giving you a clue!

Use it to find Dan. Thank me when you do.

(ZEKE *walks away.*)

ZEKE (*To himself*):

That horse is rather smart. His mind is rather slick.

His brain seems very nimble, and his delivery is quick.

But what did he mean, they go back to their nest?

I think I'd better go talk to the rest.

(ZEKE *enters.*)

ELLEN (*Surprised*):

Zeke! You're back!

ZEKE:

Yes, and I have clues!

UNCLE RICHARD:

I hope they will be helpful—something we can use.

AUNT MARTHA:

Tell us now, Zeke. Tell us what you can.

Share the information that will lead us back to Dan.

ZEKE:

Let's say a man is tired. He's all tuckered out.

Tell me, does that man still want to run about?

AUNT MARTHA:

No, he wants to rest. He doesn't want to roam.

He wants to relax in the place he calls home.

ELLEN (*Excited*)**:**

That's it! A home page! I think that Zeke is right!

We'll view our town Web page. Dan might be there tonight!

PENNY (*Excited*)**:**

It's loading.

AUNT MARTHA:

There it is—a picture of the town!

ELLEN (*Thrilled*)**:**

And look—I can see Dan walking around!

(*A loud BOOM is heard and cloud of smoke covers the computer. When the smoke clears,* DAN *is standing next to the computer.*)

ALL:

Dan!

ELLEN:

Dan! You're back! Where on earth have you been?

DAN:

I've just explored a world never seen!

UNCLE RICHARD:

Tell us your adventure. We really want to know.

Maybe, if we're lucky, someday we'll get to go.

DAN:

The Internet is amazing. I moved from page to page.

There's information for everyone, regardless of their age!

I went to sites for farmers. I learned about the soil.

I saw how others plow their fields and run their stoves
with oil!

I learned about a healthy plant that grows a solid stalk.

ZEKE:

Say, did you see anything about horses that can talk?

(*Everyone laughs.*)

THE END

Think Critically

1. Do you think the author likes or dislikes the Internet? Why?

2. Why did Uncle Richard want to search for Dan on an encyclopedia Web site?

3. How can you tell that Dan enjoyed his trip into cyberspace?

4. What is a word that means the same thing as *fiercely* does on page 7?

5. If you could be any character in this story, who would it be?

 Language Arts

Write a Poem This play rhymes! Think of a conversation that people might have and write it as a rhyming play.

School-Home Connection Discuss this play with a family member or neighbor. Then discuss how the Internet has changed the world.

Word Count: 1,150